Enough to Say It's Far

The Lockert Library of Poetry in Translation

Editorial Advisor: Richard Howard

FOR OTHER TITLES IN THE LOCKERT LIBRARY, SEE PAGE 151

Enough to Say It's Far

SELECTED

POEMS OF

PAK CHAESAM

Translated by

David R. McCann and Jiwon Shin

PRINCETON UNIVERSITY PRESS

PRINCETON AND OXFORD

Copyright © 2006 by Princeton University Press

Published by Princeton University Press, 41 William Street, Princeton,
New Jersey 08540
In the United Kingdom: Princeton University Press, 3 Market Place,
Woodstock, Oxfordshire OX20 1SY
All Rights Reserved

Library of Congress Cataloging-in-Publication Data

Pak, Chae-sam.
    [Poems. English & Korean Selections]
    Enough to say it's far : selected poems of Pak Chaesam / translated by David R.
  McCann and Jiwon Shin.
        p.   cm. — (Lockert library of poetry in translation)
    Poems in both English and Korean.
    ISBN-13: 978-0-691-12445-2 (cloth : alk. paper)
    ISBN-10: 0-691-12445-0 (cloth : alk. paper)
    ISBN-13: 978-0-691-12446-9 (pbk. : alk. paper)
    ISBN-10: 0-691-12446-9 (pbk. : alk. paper)
        I. McCann, David R. (David Richard), 1944–   II. Shin, Jiwon, 1969–
  III. Title. IV. Series
    PL992.62.C4A26   2006
    895.7'14—dc22   2005054515

British Library Cataloging-in-Publication Data is available

Publication of this book has been supported by the Sunshik Min Endowment for the
Advancement of Korean Literature, Korea Institute, Harvard University

This book has been composed in Sabon with Origami Display

Printed on acid-free paper. ∞

pup.princeton.edu

Printed in the United States of America

10 9 8 7 6 5 4 3 2 1

The Lockert Library of Poetry in Translation is supported by a bequest from
Charles Lacy Lockert (1888–1974)

Contents

❧

Acknowledgments   *xi*

Introduction   *xiii*

Soaring Dragon Waterfall   *3*

Han   *5*

Sound of the Taffy Seller's Shears   *7*

Landscape   *9*

Thousand-Year Wind   *11*

From the Song of a Celebrated Singer   *13*

A Path of a Heavenly Maiden   *15*

Autumn River in Burning Tears   *17*

Some Day, Some Month   *19*

As Summer Goes and Autumn Comes   *21*

Landscape Painter   *23*

Enough to Say It's Far   *25*

In the Wind   *27*

Contents

Waking Alone at Dawn *29*

Spring's Pathway *31*

News from Home *33*

Immortals' Paduk Game *35*

Untitled *37*

Night at Tonghak Temple *39*

Seeing the Ferry *41*

My First Love *43*

In an Empty Courtyard *45*

Nothing *47*

Seeing the Fresh Green *49*

The Feeling of the Gingko *51*

Recollection 13 *53*

Spring Path *55*

The Road Back *57*

New *Arirang* *59*

Looking at Winter Trees *61*

Contents

Spring Riverside   *63*

By the Night Sea   *65*

Having a Drink   *67*

Poplar   *69*

Friend, You Have Gone   *71*

My Poem   *73*

At the River   *75*

Recollection 18   *77*

Recollection 29   *79*

I Know the Heart of the Wildgoose   *81*

Without Title   *83*

On a Rainy Day   *85*

Tree   *87*

Autumn Sea   *89*

Flowers on a Dead Tree   *91*

Song of Death   *93*

Diary in Summer Heat   *95*

Contents

Flowers May Bloom   *97*

Four-Line Poems   *99*

   1 Brightness   *99*

   2 With One Head   *101*

   3 Place   *103*

   4 A Song   *105*

Baby's Foot on My Brow   *107*

Asking Not Understanding   *109*

What You Sent Me   *111*

P'iri Hole   *113*

Days and Months   *115*

Parenthetical   *117*

Before the Wind   *119*

What I Learned from the Sea   *121*

Looking at the Sunlight   *123*

Shimmering   *125*

Small Song   *127*

Stars   *129*

Contents

By the Mountain   *131*

As for Love   *133*

After an Illness   *135*

Going to the Mountain   *137*

Place Where I Look at Islands   *139*

Recollection 16   *141*

Autumn Coming   *143*

A Night When Sleep Is Far   *145*

Translators' Epilogue   *147*

Acknowledgments

Our thanks to Kim Cheong Lip, Mrs. Pak Chaesam, for permission to publish the original poems. The Daesan Foundation generously supported the translation project. The publication of the collection was supported by the Sunshik Min Fund, at Harvard University's Korea Institute. Special thanks to Young-Jun Lee and Hyun-Joo Yoon for their help with the preparation of the manuscript.

We wish to acknowledge Columbia University Press for permission to include nine poems by Pak Chaesam from *The Columbia Anthology of Modern Korean Poetry*, edited by David R. McCann, originally published in 2004.

INTRODUCTION

Pak Chaesam was something of a literary inside-outsider. He was born in 1933, and spent the first three years of his life in Japan, until his family moved back to Korea. His health was always frail, and he had his first hypertensive outbreak at the age of thirty-five. He grew up poor and spent most of his life struggling financially, so much so that when his deteriorating health took a fatal turn, his literary colleagues raised funds to support him. He died in 1997 of complications of kidney failure. Though well regarded in literary circles during his writing career, and the recipient of many of Korea's most prestigious literary prizes, he stayed at the edges. Rather than engagement with the social and political issues that drew the literary attentions of so many Korean writers during the 1970s and 1980s, Pak's works seem stubbornly local in subject matter, while his language pursues a nostalgic idiom, with verb forms, for example, more hesitantly reflective, delicate, and ornate, than the assertively political diction of many of his contemporaries.

Pak spent the early years of his life near Samch'ŏnp'o, a seaside town on Korea's south coast, to which his poetic imagination frequently returns. In Pak's poems, the sea is both the place of loss and bewildering abundance, because it swallows the sorrow of "flowing folds of the widow's skirts" and returns it with shimmering waves. It is with the wistfulness of a boy who grew up watching grief turning into shimmering waves that Pak Chaesam builds his poems around the yearning of all lyric verse. Beneath the iridescent waves is something lost, and Pak's poems enact the impossibility of realizing the contours of that ineffable subject. The poems begin from a place, or a point, located in the human world, a flowering branch of a tree in a courtyard, for instance, and then climb out of it into contemplation of not a vast universe, but the space that surrounds it, "Half the branches in this world, the remainder in the next." One of the first to have noticed Pak's poetic talent, a celebrated and controversial lyric poet of South Korea, the late Sŏ Chŏngju, once noted in Pak's poetry "the most exquisite expression of the Korean sense of *han*," a generalized cultural construct of melancholy or resigned resentment.

Pak was also active in Korean Paduk circles—the game with black and white stones more widely known in the West by its Japanese name Go. He wrote on the subject, edited and contributed to the major Korean journals, and was known even in Japan for his expertise. Those who know the game need not be reminded of its strategic indirection, its aesthetic of space rather than confrontation, both useful analogues to Pak Chaesam's poetics of indirection. His poems do not attack, but meander about the subjects. The poetic meandering inexorably creates distance, which, even on a subject as intimate as a desire for the beloved, designates pain of separation from what the poems speak about. Rather than speech itself, his poems attend the silence that accompanies and remains after speech or other sound. The distance that silence maps between words, sounds, or lovers becomes poetry in Pak Chaesam. This poetic distance is like having a lover's house "just over one more hill" yet just remaining there, without any attempt to cross over that distance with words. Thus we named this collection of translations after his poem "Enough to Say It's Far."

Poverty and illness were both the facts of Pak Chaesam's life and his poetic motifs. It was as if he relied on writing to turn the dreariness of enduring the physical affliction into something as surprisingly pleasant as an afternoon in reverie while watching the pot of herbal medicine boiling in the corner of the yard. Or perhaps as in the line "illness in my body lingering, like the debt that must be repaid," he seems to have made the physical affliction endurable by turning it into financial affliction. His poverty was legendary. His father was a day laborer. His mother gathered sea squirts and sold them at the markets in Samch'ŏnp'o. His uncles, fishermen, sailed to the sea and some of them never returned, leaving the aunts who followed their men by throwing themselves into the sea. His brother worked as an errand boy at a local inn, and Pak grew up chewing on the leftover food that his brother brought home from time to time. He had to delay attending middle school because the family couldn't afford the fee of a mere three thousand *wŏn*, the equivalent of less than three dollars now. Poverty, too, aches like a child's dream of "gathering up money after a day when I had gathered gingko leaves." But in Pak's poems, poverty is never sociological, neither a disabling deficiency nor social or political cause: instead, it enables lyric. It wasn't as if his poems were meant to embellish poverty. He knew too well that poems cannot do such a thing; they only modestly lessen the pain and humiliation of being poor. He wrote in the preface to his last collection of poems published in 1994:

I feel that it has been in vain, this path I've chosen: no matter how hard one tries, in the end it doesn't work out. Even so, I couldn't help but "retie the bootlaces as if starting upon something new." I just wish, in the end, it might add something to my wretched pocket. What more can I say?

Poetic fulfillment cannot be tallied; only the money that it sometimes brings can be reckoned. Surely we can count the number of publications. He wrote poems all through his adult life; they amount to fifteen published books of poems. Among his other publications are numerous books of prose essays, many of which, he would have admitted, he wrote in order to make ends meet. But in his case, the sheer number of books under his name seems deceptive in light of the destitution and isolation he endured, especially during the final years of his life. One of his admirers, who had a chance to interview him only weeks before his passing, and wrote an article about the interview, lamented the heartlessness of the literary world that would let its most faithful child suffer in neglect.

In his position at the edges of the literary world, in the delicate precision of the diction, and in his characteristic turn toward a liminal space between the present world and some other in his poetry, Pak was quite unlike some of his better publicized contemporaries in late twentieth-century Korea who wrote about violence and wrath in postcolonial and postwar Korea. That he kept a distance from subjects concerning the war is particularly surprising given the fact that he debuted in 1953, the year of the signing of the armistice of the Korean War, which sealed the border between North and South. There is no war-torn landscape in Pak's poems; just the silent hunger of a child in a breezy seaside town where even the winds merely pass by. Five out of his fifteen books of poems were published in the 1970s, the period of the authoritarian Park Chung Hee regime, the emerging labor movement, popular outcries for democracy, and general political turmoil, when a great number of his colleagues were writing protest poems and being thrown in jail. Other Korean poets have become known outside of Korea, in some part because of the more apparent connections between their poetry and either political themes having appeal to non-Korean readers, or thematic or gestural elements that manage to survive the translation process. With Pak's poetry, we feel that a riskier project has been undertaken. We are both grateful and slightly abashed at the Lockert Library's interest in this unusual, elusive, and yet ultimately rewarding project—for us, a chance to work together on the translations while yet far apart geographically, over the course of several years; and for the reader, we trust, a chance to encounter the work of a poet unlike many others from late twentieth-century Korea, yet having artistic brethren in many places.

Enough to Say It's Far

飛龍瀑布韻

하늘의 소리가 이제
땅의 소리로 화해도

雪嶽山 飛龍瀑布는
반은 아직 하늘의 것

어둘 녘 결국 밤하늘에
내맡기고 내려왔네.

Soaring Dragon Waterfall

By now the voice of the sky
may have become the voice of the earth;

half of Sŏrak Mountain's Piryong Falls
still is a part of the sky.

In the end, I left it with the evening sky
and came back down again.

恨

감나무쯤 되랴,
서러운 노을빛으로 익어가는
내 마음 사랑의 열매가 달린 나무는!

이것이 제대로 뻗을 데는 저승밖에 없는 것 같고
그것도 내 생각하던 사람의 등뒤로 뻗어가서
그 사람의 머리 위에서나 마지막으로 휘드려질까본데,

그러나 그 사람이
그사람의 안마당에 심고 싶던
느꺼운 열매가 될런지 몰라!
새로 말하면 그 열매 빛깔이
前生의 내 숯설움이요 숯소망인 것을
알아내기는 알아낼런지 몰라!
아니, 그 사람도 이 세상을
설움으로 살았던지 어쨌던지
그것을 몰라, 그것을 몰라!

4

Han

Something like the persimmon tree?
Ripening in the sad evening glow,
the tree where the fruits of my heart's love
ripen.

With room to spread in the next world only,
still it looms behind the one I was thinking of,
falling down from above her head.

It may yet become the fruit
of her overwhelming grief
that she wished to plant
in the yard of her house.
Or would she understand
if I said it was all my sorrow,
all my hope from a previous life,
the color of that fruit?
Or did that person too
live in sorrow through this world?
That I do not know, I do not know.

엿장수의 가위소리

내 몸에 아직 病도 남아 있고
갚아야 할 利子돈도 고스란히 남아 있다마는
그런 것은 이미 괜찮단다.
새 樂章을 여는
문득 엿장수의 가위소리
내 정신 풀밭에
찬란한 보석을 흩뿌리네.
햇빛하고도 제일 친한
그 엿장수의 가위소리 앞으로 가,
떼어 주는 맛뵈기 엿이나 얻어먹으면
物理가 트일 것인가, 또는
영원으로 향한 길목에 접어들었다는
슬픈 착각에라도 이르를 것인가.

Sound of the Taffy Seller's Shears

There is illness in my body lingering,
like the debt that must be repaid,
but I can deal with that.
The sudden sound of the taffy seller's shears
as they begin their new composition
scatters brilliant gems
on the grassy meadow of my mind.
If I go out into the sound of
the taffy seller's shears,
close companion to the sunlight,
and get a little piece snipped off
just to try the taste,
will the law of nature be revealed, or
will I arrive at the mistaken notion
that I have rounded the corner
toward eternity?

한 景致

풀밭에 바람이 날리듯이
남쪽바다에 햇살이 날리네.

바야흐로
갈매기 두어마리
無心끝에 날으고
돛단배 가물가물
먼 나라로 갈 듯이 떴네.

오, 안스러운 것,
하얀 하얀 저것들,
어디까지 가서야 지치는 것이랴,
지쳐서는 돌아오는 것이랴.

꽃지는 꽃그늘엔
바람이 잠시 피하고
저것들의 깃쭉지와 돛폭 아래선
햇살이 잠시 피하는가.

사람들이여
이승과 저승은 어디서 갈린다더냐.

풀밭에 바람이 흐르듯이
남쪽 바다에 햇살이 흐르네.

Landscape

The winds pass over the grassy field;
sunlight passes across the southern sea.

As two or three gulls
have risen at the end
of their indifference, a sailboat
has gone far and farther away,
as if bound for some dim and distant land.

How pitiable,
these, and these white things,
gone only so far and tiring;
and tiring, turning to come back.

For a moment the wind
finds refuge in the shadow
of the falling flower.
Beneath the wing,
or under the sail,
for a brief moment
the sunlight finds refuge.

Where do you suppose this
and the next world divide?

Winds cross the grassy fields
as sunlight passes over the southern sea.

千年의 바람

천년 전에 하던 장난을
바람은 아직도 하고 있다.
소나무 가지에 쉴새 없이 와서는
간지러움을 주고 있는 걸 보아라
아, 보아라 보아라
아직도 천 년 전의 되풀이다.

그러므로 지치지 말 일이다.
사람아 사람아
이상한 것에까지 눈을 돌리고
탐을 내는 사람아.

Thousand-Year Wind

The wind is still playing
its tricks of a thousand years ago.
See how it ceaselessly comes back
to the pine boughs and tickles them.
See, just see, what it still
goes on repeating after a thousand years.

So do not grow weary.
You, the one who
turns even to strange things
in your yearning; you.

한 名唱의 노래에서

소나무 잔가지에 어리는 바람
그 소슬한 韻처럼 임이여
나도 그대에게 그렇게 닿아가고 싶다.

그러나 이는
여든 살 道로도 안 되는 꿈
아, 그래서
살이 묻은 피가 묻은
내 財産이 목소리
갈아오던 肝臟밭
송두리째 찢어서 뽑아서
몸부림으로 바쳐 노래하노니.

From the Song of a Celebrated Singer

Wind that moves among the pine branches;
with such a gentle stirring, my love,
I wish I could go to you.

But this is a dream
that eighty years of practice will not bring.
So it is. With this flesh-stained,
blood-stained voice, my one, sole possession,
torn from the field that I
cultivate, ripped root, branch and trunk
from my innermost body
shaken to its core, I sing you
this song.

仙女의 첫길

雪嶽山 그 많은 봉우리들을 보고 있으면
仙女가 내려온 길이 보인다.
그것은 외길이 아니다,
두 갈래 세 갈래 길도 아니다,
무수하게 골지고 깊은
사타구니의 부끄러운 길,
햇살과 구름이 만났다 헤어지는 언저리,
하 엷은 옷자락 소리도 들리고
거룩한 살냄새도 난다.

A Path of a Heavenly Maiden

Seeing the many peaks of Sŏrak Mountain,
the heavenly maiden's descending path
appears. Not a single trail,
nor a path of two or three branches,
but a shy path along the inner
thighs, deepened with numerous valleys,
the borderline where clouds
and sunlight met and departed,
where the sound of thin robes rustling,
and even the scent of divine flesh
may be captured.

울음이 타는 가을江

마음도 한자리 못 앉아 있는 마음일 때,
친구의 서러운 사랑 이야기를
가을햇볕으로나 동무삼아 따라가면,
어느새 등성이에 이르러 눈물나고나.

제삿날 큰집에 모이는 불빛도 불빛이지만,
해질녘 울음이 타는 가을江을 보겄네.

저것 봐, 저것 봐,
네보담도 내보담도
그 기쁜 첫사랑 산골물소리가 사라지고
그 다음 사랑끝에 생긴 울음까지 녹아나고,
이제는 미칠 일 하나로 바다에 다 와 가는,
소리죽은 가을江을 처음 보겄네.

Autumn River in Burning Tears

When my mind cannot find a way to rest in any place,
if I follow the trail of a friend's sad story of love,
taking autumn sunlight along as a kind of companion,
before I know it I am at the ridge, and the tears come.

The lamps and other lights that gather
at elder brother's house for the ceremonies
may be lights, but I have seen the autumn river
burning in tears as the sun sets.

Look at that, just look!
                    No, more than you, more than me . . .
When the fresh and happy words of first love
like the sound of a mountain stream fade,
and even the tears that next rise
at the end of love have melted away,
I saw for the first time
the autumn river whose voice had died
as it came in its madness to the sea.

某月某日

종일을 뙤약볕에
살 깍이는 黃土재의 아픔을
곰곰 생각하며
가다간 폴폴폴 날리는
흙바람도 헤아려 보는가
아내여 그대 또한 언덕처럼
젖가슴 풀어 헤쳐 누워 있고
구름의 나들이가 보기 좋은 시방
마당 구석에는 藥湯이 끓고 있다.

Some Day, Some Month

Thinking about
the pain of the yellow earth hill
shedding its skin in the dust
of long, hot days of sunshine,
are you also considering
the wind that went flying
past past past, raising
  the dust?
My wife, just now
as you lie like that hill in the sun,
your breasts uncovered,
it seems good to be watching
the meandering clouds
while the medicine pot boils away
in the other corner of the yard.

여름 가고 가을 오듯

여름 가고
가을 오듯
해가 지고
달이 솟더니,

땀을 뿌리고
오곡을 거두듯이
햇볕 시달림을 당하고
별빛 보석을 줍더니,

아, 사랑이여
귀중한 울음을 바치고
이제는 바꿀 수 없는 노래를 찾는가.

As Summer Goes and Autumn Comes

As summer goes
and autumn comes,
the sun goes down,
the moon rises,

as sweat is scattered
and the five grains harvested,
torments of the sun endured
for the jewel moonlight to be gathered up,

O my love,
have you offered up your precious tears
in seeking a song that cannot be changed?

한 山水畫家

산 하고 물 하고 밖에는
그릴 수가 없었던 山水畫家는
차라리 새소리를 구슬로
신령한테 바쳐버리고
햇빛과 바람도 다시
바쳐버리고

아지랭이 畫筆로
멍한 귀머거리 山水를
대할 수밖에 없었다.

Landscape Painter

Once there was a landscape artist
who could paint nothing but mountains and water,
so he offered up, bead by bead, the voices of the birds
and gave them to the gods;
the sunlight, and the wind as well,
he offered up

and was left with no more than a brush
full of shimmering air
facing the deafened mountains and waters.

아득하면 되리라

해와 달, 별까지의
거리 말인가
어쩌겠나 그냥 그 아득하면 되리라.

사랑하는 사람과
나의 거리도
자로 재지 못할 바엔
이 또한 아득하면 되리라.

이것들이 다시
냉수사발 안에 떠서
어른어른 비쳐오는
그 이상을 나는 볼 수가 없어라.
그리고 나는 이 냉수를
시방 갈증 때문에
마실밖에는 다른 작정은 없어라.

Enough to Say It's Far

About the distance
to the sun and moon, to the stars,
whatever else, it is
enough to say it's far.

And the distance between
my love and me,
since it cannot be measured with a rule,
for this too
it is enough to say it's far.

I cannot see beyond
these things, afloat,
glimmering,
in the bowl of cool water.
And because of my thirst
now I have no other thought
than to drink of this cool water.

바람을 받으며

네 머리카락을
잔잔히 가르면서
아름다운 희롱으로
흐르던 바람이

내게 와서는
무슨 원수가 졌다고
왜 이렇게 허리께만
감고 돌며 쌀쌀하게 구는가.

소녀여, 너는 꿈이 있어서
그 꿈결 가까운 곳 앞머리를
무지개빛으로 수를 놓던
선연한 바람이었거늘

내 가장 쓰리고 아픈 곳
허리께를 쓰다듬어 주기는 커녕
칼날을 세우고 와서는
난도질만 하누나.

In the Wind

Parting your hair
gently, an elegant
flirtation, the wind
that passed

now
confronts me like a foe,
wraps around my
middle, chilly,
distant.

With your dream,
girl, you were once
a quick breeze,
embroidering your hair,
dreamily,
with rainbow hues;

but now here
where most sharply
I feel the pain,
you do not caress me but
whet the blade and
stab, and stab.

새벽잠 홀로 깨어

새벽잠 홀로 깨어
물같은 공기 배인 창호지 본다.

일어나기엔
허리 밑 처지는 게으름을,
다시 눈을 감기엔
눈썹 위 뜨락이 말갛게 쓸리는 상쾌함을,
그들은 시방 占三으로 장자못으로 떠나
즐거움을 낚으련만
나는 오직 창호지!

옛사랑 물에 어릴까
이 어리석은 한 때,
이도 하나 그윽한 기다림이로다.

Waking Alone at Dawn

Awakening alone at dawn
I look at the rice paper door
soaked in waterlike air.

Getting up,
laziness pulls at my waist,
or closing my eyes again,
a freshness that sweeps clean
the area above my brow:
by now they have started off
for Kosam, to Changja Pond,
and while they fish for happiness,
I am left with the rice paper door!

Is an old love to be found
in the water? Even such
an idle thought as this
might fill my empty waiting.

봄이 오는 길

얼음 풀린 강을 끼고
앓고 난 누님을 모시고...

이 두 가지를 겸하면
아리아리 저승도 가까운가.

아득한 강 건너 마을엔
복사꽃도 피어나는지

시방 잉잉거리는 벌떼소리
아지랑이 흐르고

山 이마엔 눈녹는 기척
보얗게 안개 서리고

나는 차마 손짓할 수 없다
봄이 오는 완연한 저 길을.

Spring's Pathway

Along the river where the ice has melted
in company with my sister just recovered . . .

Does serving both together
make the faint next world any clearer?

In the village away across the river,
have the peach blossoms started to bloom?

Just now the bees are birring
and the air is filled with a shimmering,

the pearly mists are rising,
a sign of the snows melting on the mountaintops,

and still I cannot point it out:
the plain, the visible pathway that spring is coming down.

고향 소식

아, 그래,
乾材藥 냄새 유달리 구수하고 그윽하던
한냇가 대실 藥局……알다 뿐인가
수염 곱게 기르고 풍채 좋던
그 노인께서 세상을 떠났다고?
아니, 그게 벌써 여러 해 됐다고?
그리고 조금 내려와서
八浦 웃동네 모퉁이
혼자 늙으며 술장사하던
蛇梁섬 昌權이 姑母,
노상 동백기름을 바르던
아, 그분 말이라, 바람같이 떴다고?

하기야 사람 소식이야 들어 무얼 하나,
끝내는 흐르고 가고 하기 마련인 것을…
그러나 가령 둔덕에 오르면
햇빛과 바람 속에서 군데군데 대밭이
아직도 그전처럼 시원스레 빛나며 흔들리고 있다든지
못물이 먼데서 그렇다든지
혹은 섬들이 졸면서 떠 있다든지
요컨대 그런 일들이 그저
내 일같이 반갑고 고맙고 할 따름이라네.

News from Home

Yes, yes: the medicine shop, Taesil,
down by the stream;
that smell, pungent, of all those dried herbs:
I know it, I know it well.
But you're saying the old man—
he had that fine, full beard
and such a sturdy build;
you say he's gone, left this life?
And it's already been several years?
And down by the corner
at P'alp'o town,
Ch'anggwŏn's auntie from Saryang island,
the one who sold wine as she got older,
the one who always used
camellia oil in her hair?
You mean her too? Gone like the wind?

What's to be made of such news?
It all winds up flowing by, passing on . . .
But if the bamboo groves up on the hill
are swaying bright and cool as before
here and there in the sunlight and wind,
and the pond waters down below are still,
the islands drowsily floating,
I can still be thankful, after all,
as if these were still my affair.

神仙바둑

바둑 한 수에는
千年이 흘러 갔는데

그 다음 한 수에는
千年이 지나도 아직

판위에 돌 떨어지는
소리가 아니 나네.

Immortals' Paduk Game

For a single move a thousand
years have gone flowing past

while for the next move a thousand
years have passed and still

no sound of a stone
striking the board.

無題

大邱 近郊 과수원
가늘고 아득한 가지

사과빛 어리는 햇살 속
아침을 흔들고

기차는 몸살인 듯
시방 한창 열이 오른다.

애인이여
멀리 있는 애인이여

이런 때는
허리에 감기는 비단도 아파라.

Untitled

In sunlight suffused
with the glow of apples

on thin distant branches
in orchards near Taegu,

morning shakes, as the train,
like an illness,
reaches the height of its fever.

Love, my love
so very far:

in moments like this
even silk round my waist is painful.

東鶴寺 一夜

눈녹은 물과 봄밤을
나란히 묻어버리면

저승 어디선가
낙숫물이 뚝뚝 지고

그대의 먼 입술가에
지금 天地가 무너진다.

Night at Tonghak Temple

Bury in order the snowmelt
and the spring night,

and somewhere in the next world
water drops fall from the eaves

while at the very edge of your faraway
lips, now the whole universe collapses.

나룻배를 보면서

저 萬丈같은 넓은 못물 위에
사람은 작은 배를 만들어
띄워보지만
결국은
물결의 반짝반짝
빛나는 영원한 무늬를
약간은 지웠다는 것만
아픈 자국이 되어 남는데.

사랑이여
나는 그대에게
가까이 가려고 한 욕심이
그대의 그지없는 조용한 가슴에
상처만 남겼느니.

Seeing the Ferry

Someone can make a small boat
and set it asail
on the vast-seeming waters
of the broad pond,
but in the end
what remains is a painful fragment,
the brief erasure
of the waves' eternal
brilliant, glittering design.

O my love,
this desire to draw
close to you has left
only that wound
in your boundless
and patient heart.

첫사랑 그 사람은

첫사랑 그 사람은
입맞춘 다음엔
고개를 못 들었네.
나도 딴 곳을 보고 있었네.

비단올 머리칼
하늘 속에 살랑살랑
햇미역 냄새를 흘리고,
그 냄새 어느덧
마음 아파라,
내 손에도 묻어 있었네.

오, 부끄러움이여, 몸부림이여,
골짜기에서 흘려 보내는
실개천을 보아라,
물비늘 쓴 채 물살은 울고 있고,
우는 물살 따라
달빛도 포개어진 채 울고 있었네.

My First Love

My first love, she
could not lift her face
after the kiss.
And I was looking
somewhere else as well.

Silken strands of her hair
scented soft as the newly
picked seaweed in the air;
that scent so soon
causing the heart to ache
has attached itself
to my hand.

Oh the shame, the writhing!
Look at the slender stream
sent down out of the valley,
how in their watery scales
the currents make their weeping,
and moonlight, after the currents,
piled on top was weeping too.

不在

다 나가고 없는 뜰에
木蓮花가 피었네.

반쯤은 가지를 이승에
나머지는 저승에

골고루 사람이 없는 데 따라
고이 여는 꽃이여!

In an Empty Courtyard

In a courtyard that all have left,
magnolias are in bloom.

Half the branches
in this world, the remainder in the next,

flower quietly wherever
places are away from human habitation.

無心

가다간 파초잎에
바람이 불어오고

덩달아 물방울이
찬란하게 튕기고

無心한 이 한때 위에
없는 듯한 세상을.

Nothing

Sometimes the wind
blows over the plantain leaf

where the drops of water
take their bright form, and fall.

Beyond this moment of perfect calm
life wants nothing.

新綠을 보며

나는 무엇을 잘못했는가.

바닷가에서 자라
꽃게를 잡아 함부로 다리를 분질렀던 것,
생선을 낚아 회를 쳐 먹었던 것,
햇빛에 반짝이던 물꽃무늬 물살을 마구 헤엄쳤던 것,
이런 것이 一時에 수런거리며 밑도 끝도 없이 대들어 오누나.

또한 이를 달래 창자 밑에서 일어나는 微風
가볍고 연한 현기증을 이기지 못하누나.

아, 나는 무엇을 이길 수가 있는가.

Seeing the Fresh Green

What things have I done wrong?

Having grown up by the sea,
caught crabs and without much thought,
snapped off their legs,
turned fish I hooked
into sashimi and ate it raw,
swam heedlessly through the flowering patterns
of sunlight gleaming on the waves:
such things as these all at once
well up, bottomless, endless, confronting me.

And to soothe these, the gentle tremor that rises
deep within; the light and gentle vertigo,
something I cannot overcome.

What is there that I can ever overcome?

은행잎 感傷

내 熱病도 가실 겸
지난번 고향길에는
金融組合 뒷뜰에 가
은행잎을 보면서 새 눈물을 배웠네.

은행잎을 줍던 날 밤은
돈을 줍던 꿈으로
홀로 쓸쓸한 小學生이었던가.

은행 한잎을
修身책에 꽂고서
돈 생각이 나을까
공부생각이 나을까.

나는 선생님 앞에
많은 아이와 함께 은행잎 되어
자꾸 자꾸 손을 드는 것이다
네, 네, 네, 네, 네……
황금의 눈물을
가을 땅바닥에 지우며 나는 섰어라.

The Feeling of the Gingko

That last time on my way home
I had gone to ease the fever.
I went into the yard behind
the credit union office
and I learned a new form
of tears, looking at the gingko leaves.

As a primary school student,
lonely and unhappy, I had dreamed
of gathering up money after a day
when I had gathered gingko leaves.

Which was it, money
or my studies that I thought of
when I placed one gingko leaf
between the pages of our ethics book?

With all the other children
I became a gingko leaf myself,
there in front of the teacher,
steadily raising our hands
as she counted Yes, yes, yes, yes . . .

Scattering tears of yellow gold,
I stood there on the autumn ground.

追憶에서 13

해수욕을 하고 나면
닦을 수건도 없이
고추를 내놓고 몸을 말렸다.
더운 날도 가다간 새파라니
얼어서 추워 오곤 했었다.
동네의 누가 보건
하나 아랑곳이 없었다.
실은 누님 친구들이랑
아주머니뻘 되는 여자들이 봐도
부끄러움도 없이 예사로
고추를 내놓고 해바라기를 해 가며
아득한 시간을 보냈다.
그러나 어린 여자아이들은
고추도 없으련만
연방 감추기만 하고
더 쑥스러워하는 것은
그 까닭을 알 수 없었다.
달랑달랑 무슨
요령소리라도 날 듯이
고추를 단 것이
자랑스럽기조차 했다.

Recollection 13

After a dip in the sea
without towels
we would dry off,
our peppers showing plainly.
Even on hot days
they sometimes were cold
and we seemed to freeze, pale.
When big sister's friends
or some auntie saw us,
why, quite without shame
we just sat there letting time
go by, our peppers showing,
like a row of sunflowers.
But we couldn't understand the girls,
why, without little peppers
to hide they still covered themselves,
shy and afraid.
We might have been a bit
too proud of our peppers
as they jingle-jangled
like handbells.

봄길

봄 나뭇가지, 이를테면
수양버들을 오르던 물기운이
이제는 눈부신 공기 그것이 되어
"여보게 기운을 내게, 기운을 내!" 한다.
나는 허울을 벗은 한 마리 벌레
지금은 땅을 기고 있지만
나중엔 뛰다가 날으다가 할 것을,

이 나긋나긋한 손발과 등살과
그리고 가슴에 눈에
그것은 너무 벅차고 짐스럽고나.
"여보게 기운을 내게, 기운을 내!"
실로 九十春光은 너무 바빠
당할 수 없는 괴로움에
기어가다가 쉬다가,
아지랭이로 누워서 흐르는
하루해 길다.

Spring Path

Spring boughs, or to be more precise,
the force of the moisture rising
through the weeping willow now turns
into dazzling air and speaks. It says,
"You, there! Pull yourself together, you!"
I am an insect that has molted.
Though I crawl on the ground I shall be
leaping, later, and flying.

But for now, for such painfully tender
hands and feet, back, even these eyes,
it is all too much, too burdensome, this
"You! Pull yourself together."
The ninety days of spring is a span too short
for enduring such discomfort,
so the day's light lingers on
in the crawling and the resting,
the lying down like flowing mist.

어떤 歸路

새벽 서릿길을 밟으며
어머니는 장사를 나가셨다가
촉촉한 밤이슬에 젖으며
우리들 머리맡으로 돌아오셨다.

선반엔 꿀단지가 채워져 있기는 커녕
먼지만 부옇게 쌓여 있는데,
빚으로도 못 갚는 땟국물같은 어린 것들이
방안에 제 멋대로 뒹굴어져 자는데,

보는 이 없는 것,
알아주는 이 없는 것,
이마 위에 이고 온
별빛을 풀어놓는다.
소매에 묻히고 온
달빛을 털어놓는다.

The Road Back

Starting on the frosty path at dawn,
Mother now soaked from the heavy night's dew;
Mother has come back after a day of selling
to the place where we lie asleep.

There is no jar of honey on the shelf,
only the gray dust piling,
while we children, too small and dirty to work
off the debts, lie stretched out here, there.

No one to see, no one
to comprehend when she unties
the starlight she carries back on her forehead,
and shakes loose the moonlight
that clings to her sleeves.

新 아리랑

바다 두고 산을 두고
사랑이여, 너를 버릴 수는 없을지니라.

백리 바깥을 보는
네 山처럼 아득한 눈을 어찌하고,

내 잘못을 거울처럼 받아 비추는
물같은 이마를 어찌하고,

복사꽃 피는 앵도꽃 피는
정다운 동네어구 입술을 어찌하고,

우거진 숲이여
네 시원한 머리카락을 어찌하고,

아, 어찌하고 어찌하고
고향의 稜線 젖가슴을 어찌하고,

바다 있기에 산이 있기에
사랑이여, 너를 버릴 수는 없을지니라

New *Arirang*

Granted there are mountains, granted, the sea;
but, my love, I can never leave you.

No matter what I try,
eyes distant as your mountains
that look out a hundred *li* or more;

whatever I do,
the forehead clear as water
that reflects my transgressions like a mirror;

whatever shall I do,
your lips, the warmly welcoming entrance
to the village, all blooming with peach blossoms and cherry;

and the thickly grown forest,
your cool and fragrant hair,
what shall I do?

The breasts of the hills back home,
Oh no matter what I do,
whatever I try,

because the sea and the mountain
are, my love, there is no way ever to forget you.

Arirang: the most well-known Korean folksong, having a wide range of
melodies and verses.

겨울나무를 보며

스물 안팎 때는
먼 수풀이 온통 산발을 하고
어지럽게 흔들어
갈피를 못잡는 그리움에 살았다
숨가쁜 나무여 사랑이여.

이제 마흔 가까운
손등이 앙상한 때는
나무들도 전부
겨울나무 그것이 되어
잎사귀들을 떨어내고 부끄럼 없이
시원하게 벗을 것을 벗어버렸다.

비로소 나는 탕에 들어앉아
그것들이 나를 향해
손을 흔들며
기쁘게 다가오고 있는 것 같음을
부우연 노을 속 한 경치로서
조금씩 확인할 따름이다.

Looking at Winter Trees

Until the age of twenty
I had lived in such longing,
senseless as the grove of trees
dizzily shaking its long hair
loose; O
breathless tree, O love!

Now nearing forty,
the backs of my hands thin and bony,
and the trees as well
have become winter trees, shamelessly
shedding their leaves.
They have taken off all that feels good
to take off.

And now as I settle
into the bath, I see
them drawing bit by bit
more gladly near, waving
their hands at me, the landscape
taking form in the mist and evening glow,
as if in affirmation.

봄 江邊

解産한 아내의 젖줄기
江이 흐르고,
눈이 부시고,
正面으로는 바라볼 수 없고,
딱딱한 뼈마디
죄 지은 근처
아지랑이 아른대고,
손짓조차 할 수 없고,
파릇이 풀잎에 오르는 물기운
아, 수만 마디의 말을 참는다.

Spring Riverside

Having given birth, my wife,
the flow of her breast
is a river, it
dazzles the eye,
I cannot look straight at it;
that aching bone joint
neighborhood where the sin occurred
is hidden, obscured by haze;
I cannot point to it,
the water's force rising into verdant grasses
while I bite back ten thousand
more things that I would say.

밤 바다에서

누님의 치맛살 곁에 앉아
누님의 슬픔을 나누지 못하는 심심한 때는,
골목을 빠져나와 바닷가에 서자.

비로소 가슴 울렁이고
눈에 눈물 어리어
차라리 저 달빛 받아 반짝이는 밤바다의 質定할 수 없는
괴로운 꽃비늘을 닮아야 하리.
天下에 많은 할말이, 天上의 많은 별들의 반짝임처럼
바다의 밤물결되어 찬란해야 하리.
아니 아파야 아파야 하리.

이윽고 누님은 섬이 떠 있듯이 그렇게 잠들리.
그때 나는 섬가에 부딪치는 물결처럼
누님의 치맛살에 얼굴을 묻고
가늘고 먼 울음을 울음을
울음 울리라.

By the Night Sea

At my sister's side, sitting by her skirt,
restless at the edge of her sorrow,
I want to get beyond the alleyways to stand by the sea.

When my heart's ache
and in my eyes the tears
well up, I would become more like the numberless,
the sharp flower scales shimmering in moonlight on the sea.
Many words to be said, under the sky.
Like the glitter of many stars in the sky,
let them become waves on the night sea and shine,
brilliant; or perhaps they must ache.

Soon my sister would be asleep, adrift, like the islands.
I would bury my face in my sister's skirt
like the small waves that come ashore the island,
and cry out the faint and distant cries they made.

술을 들면

술을 들면 그 술끼가
내 몸을 빙빙 몇 바퀴 돌고 나서
많이는 이 세상에 떠돌아 다녔었네.

겨우 술힘이나 빌려
그대 옆에 가는
이 못난 짓마저도
그대는 아마 모르고 있으리.

시방 내 집 뜰에 핀 라일락은
그 향기를 담 너머에까지
부지런히 흘려 보내나니.

Having a Drink

Having a drink, that drink
spun my body several times around,
to wander away through the world.

You may not know
my ill-favored gesture here
to draw close to your side
relied more than a little bit
upon the strength a drink might lend.

The lilac now blossoming in my yard
works away assiduously
to send its scent over the top of the wall.

미류나무

어젯밤에는
별을 줍던 네 눈에
오늘은
미류나무 잎사귀에서
햇빛과 바람이
어른어른 짜울린
비단을 줍고나, 구슬을 줍고나.

햇빛을 등질 수 없고
바람을 외면할 수 없는
한낮의 미류나무에서
너는 시방 너의 흩어진
머리카락을 쓸어 올리다가
짝짝이 입성을 거두다가
별짓을 다 하고 있지만,
아, 네가 선 그 곳은
이승 저 쪽도
저승 이 쪽도 아닌
혼령만 남은 자리인 줄을 모르고나.

Poplar

In your eyes where
I gathered stars last night,
today I gather
the silks and beads on poplar leaves
woven by the glimmering sunlight and winds.

Under the midday poplar
where you can neither avoid the sunlight
nor turn away from the wind,
you might brush back your straying hair,
click your tongue,
fiddling at any thing,
quite unaware
where you stood is neither
the near end of that world
nor the far end of this,
but the place where its spirit stays.

친구여 너는 가고

친구여 너는 가고
너를 이 세상에서 볼 수 없는 대신
그 그리움만한 중량의 무엇인가가 되어
이승에 보태어지는가,
나뭇잎이 진 자리에는 마치
그 잎사귀의 중량만큼 바람이
가지끝에 와 머무누나

내 오늘 설령
글자의 숲을 헤쳐
가락을 빚는다 할손
그것은 나뭇가지에 살랑대는
바람의 그윽한 그것에는
비할래야 비할 바 못되거늘,
이 일이 예삿일이 아님을
친구여 너가 감으로 뼈속 깊이 저려 오누나.

Friend, You Have Gone

Friend, you have gone,
and I wonder if in place of not being able to see you
something else might come to balance the weight
of that longing.
Where leaves have fallen,
just that weight of wind will linger
at the very tips of the boughs.

So today I push
my way through a forest of letters
to shape verses, knowing well
there is no comparing them
to the wind's still lingering
in the branches of the tree.
My friend, your leaving causes me
to feel deep in my bones
there is nothing of the ordinary about this.

나의 詩

햇빛에 반짝반짝 윤이 나고, 파랗고,
또한 빛나는 것밖에 할 줄을 모르는
저 연약한 잎사귀들을 보아라.
산들바람에 몸을
이리 눕혔다 저리 눕혔다
생명의 光輝만을 이 세상에
즐거운 노래로써 남기는,
그러나 그 한때 뿐,
가장 귀한 짓을 하면서
결국은 그냥 사라져가는
끝없는 無慾을 하염없이 바라보노라니
오히려 부끄럽고 허전하고나

나는 詩를 쓰기는 쓴다마는,
하여간 죽고나서 이 세상에
남는 것을 바라고 기록한다마는,
저 이파리의
서늘하고도 그윽한 것에 미치지 못하고
빈약하고 헛된 짓만 하는 듯
마음 절로 외로워지느니.

My Poem

There; see:
the leaves that know
nothing beyond reflection,
gleaming bright green
in the sunlight.
In soft winds they lay their bodies
some this way, some that,
leaving as a glad song
only life's brilliance in this world.
But it is only that once,
that most precious act at the end
simply vanishing. Observing
such complete absence of desire,
I feel empty, ashamed.

I write poems.
I record what I hope
will be left behind in this world
after I have died and gone,
but unable to attain the coolness and depth
of those leaves,
the empty vanity of the act
undoes me.

江물에서

무거운 짐을 부리듯
江물에 마음을 풀다.
오늘, 안타까이
바란 것도 아닌데
가만히 아지랭이가 솟아
아뜩하여지는가.

물오른 풀잎처럼
새삼 느끼는 보람,
꿈같은 그 세월을
아른아른 어찌 잊으랴,
하도한 햇살이 흘러
눈이 절로 감기는데...

그날을 돌아보는
마음은 너그럽다.
반짝이는 江물이사
주름살도 아닌 것은,
눈물이 아로새기는
내 눈부신 자욱이여!

At the River

Like setting down a heavy burden
I unbind my heart by the river.
Today I was not anxious
for it, and the shimmering air
left me dizzy.

Feeling the press of life
like the grass blade filled with its sap,
I remember the flickering
passing of dreamlike hours,
while the sun floods down so
my eyes close themselves . . .

Heart that looks back on days such as this
grows generous, opens.
Shimmering of the river
is not wrinkled skin
but my dazzling trace
that tears have chaliced.

追憶에서 18

앞바다 호수와 같은
잔잔하고 조용한 물결을 자나새나 보면서
한 자락은 여기에 펼쳤지만
다른 여러 자락은
太平洋 大西洋 印度洋을 적시고
대부분의 우리가 못 가 보고 마는
南極海 北極海에까지
잇닿아 있다는 생각을 했다.
그것은 想像力이 파악한 것이 아니라
빤한 現實追求로 따져서 그랬다.
이것을 어릴 때는
혼자만 그렇게 안 것인 양
또 마치 큰 발견인 양
아무도 몰래 쉬쉬 하는 가운데
나만 홀로 보배를 가진 것처럼 했다.
아무것도 아닌
그러면서 빛나는 冠을 머리에 쓴
이 신기한 꿈을 가졌길래
세상은 화려할 수 있었고
누구에게나 의젓하고 떳떳할 수 있었던
이것이 확실히 문제다.

Recollection 18

Watching the waves
still and quiet as a lake, day and night,
I thought of how one corner of the sea unfolds
right here, and others to moisten the Pacific,
Atlantic, Indian Ocean; and even Arctic and Antarctic,
places where most of us will never go.
Not something imagination can grasp,
but something reality discloses.
In my childhood I kept it hidden from all others,
a treasure I alone had discovered
and I alone knew. Possession
of so magical though trivial a dream
put a brilliant crown on my young head.
The whole world might be splendid, then,
and I as worthy, as honorable as any.

追憶에서 29

바지는 입어도 고추가 새파라니 언 채
바닷가 언덕에서 전쟁놀이를 했다.
콧물은 얼룩이 지게 소매 끝으로 닦으며
어둠이 서로의
얼굴 윤곽을 지우도록까지.
그 더러움을 저마다 집으로 가져 가서
어머니의 사랑으로 지우게 했다.
요컨대 학교에 들기 전
우리는 하루해가 다 가는 것이 아까왔었다.
그 신나게 놀던 창이랑 칼은
어디 으슥한 풀덤불 속에 숨기고
그것을 큰 비밀인 양 안고
아무한테도 들키지 않기를 은근히 바랐다.
지금도 나는 그런 꿈을 꾸고 있지만
아름다움이 한 발자국도 거기에서
못 나갔음을 새삼 발견하는 이 아픔이여.

Recollection 29

Our little peppers frozen white inside our pants,
we played war games on the hillside by the sea.
Wiping our runny noses, our sleeves were stained;
we played until the dark erased the outlines of our faces.
The stains we brought home for our mothers' care to clean.
Too young for school, we grew resentful of the setting sun.
Hiding spears and swords somewhere in the bushes,
their location our secret, we hoped no one would discover
  them.
I dream about such things even now, and know
that beauty has not moved a step onward from there.

그 기러기 마음을 나는 안다

기러기에게는 찬 하늘 서릿발이 아니다.
진실로 쓰리고 아픈 것은
공중에서도 강을 건너는 일이다.
무엇으로도 막을 수 없는 滔滔한
저 順理와 같은 강을 질러가는 일이다.

그러한 기러기
그 기러기 마음을 나는 안다.

나는 시방
하늘 이불을 덮은
하늘의 아기 같은 아기가 자는 옆에서
인생이 닳아버린 내 숨소리가 커서
하마하마 깨울까 남몰래 두렵느니라.

I Know the Heart of the Wildgoose

For the wildgoose, it is not the frosty coldness
of the skies. What truly
causes pain, what hurts
even in the emptiness of air
is the crossing of rivers,
cutting across the river rushing
on, unstoppable as reason itself.

Such geese;
I know the heart of such geese.

Now by the side
of a sleeping child,
heaven's own child
covered with heaven's comforter,
I worry that the sound of my breathing,
worn down in life,
may yet be so loud it will wake her.

無題

드디어 머무는 곳이라곤 없고
모두 다 떠나는 것만이네.
물결도 배도
그 위에 탄 사람도
먼 나라로 갔네.
세상은 한정없이
滅亡만이 이어져
그것이 總和가 되어
不滅의 탑을 세웠네.
가장 약한 것이
무수하게 모여서는
가장 강한 것이 되는
그 未知數를 삼삼하게 느끼네.

Without Title

In the end there is nothing that lingers;
it is all departing.
The waves, a boat,
those who ride above,
all gone off to a distant land.
Endlessly the world
becomes ruins that
accumulate, piling up
a tower of immortality.
How mysteriously
the numberless weak come together
to make the most powerful.

비오는 날에

지금, 시퍼런 칼날의 絶壁 끝에서는 빗방울은 분명
떨리며 내리고들 있을 것인데,

그리고 흔들리는 珠簾 밖 안개 속에 서 있는 우뚝
한 우뚝한 도적놈을 느끼는 것인데,

절로는 허리띠 풀리어 시름겨운 마음은 어느 새
임의 마음에 하 그리 가까이 설레어지느니라.

On a Rainy Day

Now the drops of rain at the dark knife-edge of the cliff
must be trembling as they fall,

and outside the swinging bead curtain, tall in the fog,
I can sense it, the looming presence of the thief,

and my anxious heart, as if a sash had loosened,
so quickly does it draw so trembling close to my lover's.

나무

바람과 햇빛에
끊임없이 출렁이는
나뭇잎의 물살을 보아라

사랑하는 이여,
그대 스란치마의 물살이
어지러운 내 머리에 닿아
노래처럼 풀려 가는 근심,
그도 그런 것인가.

사랑은 만 번을 해도 미흡한 渴症,
물거품이 한없이 일고
그리고 한없이 스러지는 허망이더라도
아름다운 이여,
저 흔들리는 나무의
빛나는 사랑을 빼면
이 세상엔 너무나 할 일이 없네.

Tree

Look at the ceaseless
rippling of the
leaves in sunlight,
in the wind.

Beloved, are they
like the worries
let loose as a song,
the waves of your long skirts
that reach my dizzy head?

Love is an unquenchable thirst.
Though it may rise up
endlessly, as bubbles that vanish
endlessly into empty futility,
most beautiful one:
without the love brilliantly
swaying that tree, there would not be
much else to do in this world.

가을바다

한 노래의 자지러진 가락에서 풀리어
물이 듣는 완곡한 대목에 이르듯
가을 바다는 있고나.

머리위 은행잎들은
반짝이는 노릇 만으로
시방 햇볕 쪽에 편 들고
가을 바다 쪽으로도 편 들어
꿈결 옆을 스치는데

내 속病 또한
은행잎 쪽으로도
가을 바다 쪽으로도
쏠리어 흔들려
소리하는 법 하나 배우고 있네

Autumn Sea

As if let loose from the song's most exquisite note
to reach some gentle hollow place where water drips,
the autumn sea finds itself.

In their brilliance, gingko leaves
above my head at times seem to side with the sun,
at times with the autumn sea,
brushing the dream's edge,

while the illness inside me,
wavering toward the gingko leaves,
or trembling in the autumn sea's direction,
studies one way to sing.

죽은 나무에 꽃피는

죽은 나무에 꽃피는
그 비밀을 알기 위하여

나는 예까지 왔네
그러나 알송달송한 것밖에 없고

하늘에 구름 한 송이
피었다가 지는 그 이유를 모르듯이

저 부푼 젖몽오리에서
아프게 木蓮이 피기 시작한 오늘

진정 내일을 예비하기 위하여
다른 가지를 시방 열었느니라.

Flowers on a Dead Tree

To learn the secret
why flowers bloom on a dead tree

I came all the way here.
But it's all quite unfathomable,

like the reason a cloud blossoms
and then falls apart in the sky.

From the swelling breast of the bud
today, a magnolia painfully blossoms

while in readying for tomorrow
truly, a different branch bears.

죽음의 노래

물 위에 햇빛과 바람이 어리듯이
혹은 모시옷 서늘하게 살에 닿듯이
그렇게 아련히 오는 것인가,
혹은 또 박살나는 高速버스 事故와도 같이
무서운 번개빛으로 닥치는 것인가,
아, 우리네 죽음.

그 많은 웃음자리를, 술자리를, 여자를,
또 수천 판의 바둑판 재미를
억울하게 뒷전하는 모든 섭섭함을
친구여, 낸들 왜 모르겠나.

그러나 나는 그런 것도 외면하고
잘도 하루하루 넘기지만,
혼자 깬 새벽 서너時에는
옆자리의 妻子들 잠을 저만치 밀어두고
아직도 고운 때가 묻은 채 健在한 그 죽음을
고마움과 부끄러움으로 엮어진 念珠로써 헤아린다네.

Song of Death

Does it come gently,
like ramie cloth softly touching the cool skin,
or as sunlight and wind hovering above the water?
Or is our death
sudden and frightening as a lightning flash,
like a highway bus crash, smashing everything to pieces?

Friend, I know what the unhappiness would be,
to have to leave behind the laughter,
the drinks, women, and the pleasures
of endless rounds of Paduk.

I turn away
and make it through reasonably well,
day by day; but waking at three
or four in the morning,
and pushing aside, just that much,
the wife and child who sleep beside,
I work over this death, how it
thrives, still, in its coating of fine dust,
while I count the beaded necklace
woven of gratitude and shame.

酷暑日記

잎 하나 까딱 않는
三十 몇 度의 날씨 속
그늘에 앉았어도
소나기가 그리운데
막혔던 소식을 뚫듯
매미 울음 한창이다.

계곡에 발 담그고
한가로운 부채질로
성화같은 더위에
달래는 것이 전부다.
예닐곱 적 아이처럼
물장구를 못치네.

늙기엔 아직도 멀어
靑春이 萬里인데
이제 갈 길은
막상 얼마 안 남고
그 바쁜 조바심 속에
絶壁만을 두드린다.

Diary in Summer Heat

Not a leaf moves
in this ninety-degree heat.
In the shade, longing
for a bit of some passing shower.
The cicadas racketing away
like a burst of sudden news.

This heat
comes down like a spell
of anger: all I can do
is soak my feet in the valley stream
and listlessly wave a fan
to ease it; no more
playing like a child of six or seven
in the water.

A long way yet from being old,
with miles left of youth,
worried still that the road ahead
is not that far to go. I keep time
by beating on the steep cliff.

꽃이 피어도

꽃이 피어도
고향에 못 가보고
파랗게 천지가 녹음에 덮여도
마음대로 안되는 이 일을 어쩔꺼나.

빚에 쫄려서도
시간이 없어서도 아닌
내 인생은 멎어서
겨우 원고지 칸이나 메우고
네모난 바둑판을 살피고
하루하루를 지낸다.

그 원고지 칸에
그 바둑판에 문득
철썩철썩 왔다가 부서지는
울렁거리며 살아 있는 파도가
아, 고향을 그려보게
쟁쟁쟁 소리하는
이 미칠 것 같은 한낮.

Flowers May Bloom

Flowers may bloom
but I cannot return home to see;
though all the world lies covered in its soft green,
there's nothing to be done where I cannot do as I wish.

It's not that my life
is eaten away by debts
or stripped of its hours,
but I spend it, day by day,
struggling to put words into the squares
on the writing pad, or gazing
at the empty spaces on the Paduk board.

Those squares on the paper,
spaces on the board—of a sudden,
bursting, flooding in, the waves, alive,
shout Just *picture* your home! The voice
flares up this mad midday.

四行詩 1

光明

물가에 오면 눈물나는 햇빛
눈물나는 바람 눈물나는 공기뿐이더라.
아가야 너를 데리고 오면
내 눈물에 막혀 손짓할 데 없음이여.

Four-Line Poems 1

Brightness

At the water's edge there is nothing but
sunlight that causes tears; wind; and air
that does so too. Child, when I bring you here,
holding back tears I have nothing I can point to.

四行詩 2

머리 하나로

옷벗은 구름이여.
너는 늘 내 정신 中天에 떴다.
몸뚱이는 다 달아나고 이제는 어리석게
머리 하나로 네게 닿아 가리라.

Four-Line Poems 2

With One Head

O cloud undressed,
you float always midair in my spirit.
My body has run off, so now, foolish,
I shall draw near you with only my head.

四行詩 3

어느 座席

너는 멋들어진 散調 한 曲을 튕기며
손가락이 絃이 있고 없는 것 사이를 더듬었다.
나는 지금 이 한때
내 마음이 있고 없는 지를 더듬을 수 없음이여.

Four-Line Poems 3

Place

As you play the delightful melody,
your fingers trace between where strings are or not.
At this very moment there is no tracing
if my mind is here or not.

四行詩 4

小曲

사과汁과 綠汁을 마시면
내 피를 얼마나 맑힐 것인가,
高血壓 피 그늘에 앉은 나는
그 피를 다스릴 길 없어 고개 휘어지노니.

Four-Line Poems 4

A Song

Drinking apple and vegetable juice, I wonder
how much it will clear my blood.
Seated in the shadow of high blood pressure,
with no way to cure it I let my neck bend down.

아기 발바닥에 이마 대고

一년 五개월짜리
祥圭의 잠자는 발바닥
골목 안과 뜰 안을 종일
위험하게 잘도 걸어다녔구나.
발바닥 밑으로 커다란 해를 넘긴
어여쁘디 어여쁜 발아.
돌자갈 깔린 길보다도 험한
이 애비의 이마를 한번 밟아 다오.
때 안 타는 연한 발아.

Baby's Foot on My Brow

Two-year-old Sang-gyu,
asleep now
after toddling perilously about
the alleyway and courtyard
all day; your pretty feet
that crossed over the huge sun
beneath their soles:
Here, just once try a step
on your father's forehead,
steeper even than the gravel road.
Such soft, undirtied feet.

세상을 몰라 묻노니

아무리 눈으로 새겨 보아도
별은 내게는
모가 나지 않네
그저 휘황할 뿐이네.

사랑이여 그대 또한
아무리 마음으로 그려 보아도
종잡을 수 없네
그저 뿌듯할 뿐이네.

이슬같은 목숨인 바에야
별을 이슬같이 볼까나.
풀잎같은 목숨일 바에야
사랑을 풀잎같이 볼까나.

진실로 진실로
세상을 몰라 묻노니
별을 무슨 모양이라 하겠는가.
또한 사랑을 무슨 형체라 하겠는가.

Asking Not Understanding

However intently I look,
stars to me
have no points.
They are simply, unsurpassedly brilliant.

My love, you also;
however I may seek to draw
you in my heart, I cannot capture the essence
of what simply fills me.

Should stars be seen as the dew
for having a dewlike life?
Or love seen as a grass blade
for having a grasslike existence?

Truly I do not
understand this world
and so I ask:
What shape can a star be said to have?
What form does love take?

그대가 내게 보내는 것

못물은 찰랑찰랑
넘칠 듯하면서 넘치지 않고
햇빛에 무늬를 주다가
별빛 보석도 만들어 낸다.

사랑하는 사람아,
어쩌면 좋아!
네 눈에 눈물 괴어
흐를 듯하면서 흐르지 않고
혼백만 남은 미류나무 잎사귀를,
어지러운 바람을,
못견디게 내게 보내고 있는데!

What You Sent Me

Waters in the pond, rippling
as if about to overflow,
do not flow over, but weaving
patterns in the sunlight,
craft starlight jewels as well.

My love, just
what should I do now?
The tears that gather in your eye
about to fall do not fall;
I cannot bear it.
They send me the ghosts of poplar leaves,
they send me the dizzying winds.

피리 구멍

햇빛은 제일 많이
나뭇잎과 강물에 와서는
놀다 가는 모양이더라
달빛 또한 그런 모양이더라.

그런 하염없는 세상에,
나는 그들의 사돈의 팔촌이나 되던가

부모 섬기고 형제 위하기
한결 얼룩진 무늬가 드디어
살에 패인 피리 구멍 되어
뿌리 젖은 나무로 우느니
또한 발 적시는 강물로 우느니.

P'iri Hole

It appeared
the way sunlight plays
most upon leaves and the river's surface.
Or the way moonlight has just that appearance.

In just such an idle life,
I may have become something like their distant cousin.

Serving my parents, for my brothers and sisters,
a dappled pattern becomes at last
the *p'iri* hole sunk deep in the flesh
and it sings, it sings in the drenched root of the tree,
or in the river's waters that drench the feet.

P'iri: a small reed instrument with a piercing nasal tone.

日月속에서

산은 항상 말이 없고
강은 골짜기에 갈수록 소리내어 흐른다.
이 두 다른 갈래가
그러나 조화를 이루어
얼굴이 다르지만 화목한 營爲로
나가고 있음을 본다.
세상이 생기고부터
짜증도 안내고 그런다.
이 가을 햇빛 속에서
단풍빛으로 물든 산은
높이 솟아 이마가 한결 빛나고
강물은 이리저리 몸을 뒤틀며
반짝이는 노릇만으로
그들의 존재를 없는 듯이 알리나니
이 千篇一律로 똑같은
체바퀴같은 되풀이의 日月 속에서
그러나 언제나 새로움을 열고 있는
이 비밀을 못 캔 채
나는 드디어 나이 오십을 넘겼다.

Days and Months

The mountains say nothing, ever,
while the river natters along,
flowing down through the valley.
The two different branches
have found peace, and carry on
amicably, despite the differences
in their faces.
Since time began
they have managed without grumbling.
In this autumn sun,
as light shines from the high brow
of the red-leaf-colored mountain,
and the river turns and twists
its body, their sparkling roles
tell of their existence.
In the monotonous,
ferris wheel cycle of days and months,
still unable to find the secret
of constantly new beginnings,
I have at last passed my fiftieth year.

虛無의 큰 괄호 안에서

꽃이나 잎은
아무리 아름답게 피어도
오래 가지 못하고
결국은 지고 만다.

그런데도 그 滅亡을 알면서
연방 피어서는
야단으로 아우성을 지른다.

다시 보면 限定이 있기에
더 안스럽고
더 가녀린 것인데, 그러나
위태롭게, 아프게, 이 세상에
끝없이 充滿해 있는 놀라움이여.

아, 사람도 그 榮光이
물거품 같은 것인 데도 잠시
虛無의 큰 괄호 안에서 빛날 뿐이다.

Parenthetical

Flower or leaf,
however beautifully,
it blooms not long,
and dies.

Knowing their certain ruin,
still they bloom steadily away,
making their noisy hubbub.

Though it may seem feeble
or sad, all
happening within that set limit,
that it goes on so painfully,
so perilously, is a cause
of endless astonishment.

And of course man and his glory
are but foam; yet for the moment
they gleam in the great parenthetical
emptiness.

바람 앞에서

지난 겨울에는
발을 구르는 섭섭함을 외면하고
바람은 친구를 안고
땅밑으로 땅밑으로 기어들더니

이제는 따로
새 정신이 들었는지
할미꽃 모가지를 타고 올라와
목숨이 좋다고
목숨 있는 것 근처에서만
喜喜樂樂하는고나.

바람아 바람아
네 앞에서 나는 늘
앞이 캄캄해진다.

Before the Wind

Last winter the wind
heedless of my wrenching grief
took my friend
and crawled down into the ground,
into the ground.

But now
with some renewed spirit
it climbs the stalks of anemone.
Happy with life,
wherever there is life
it breaks forth in jubilation.

O wind, wind:
before you, always
my way is dark, unknown.

바다에서 배운 것

고향 앞바다에는
꿈이 아니라고 흔드는
수만 잎사귀의 미류나무도 있고,
미칠만하게 흘러내리는
과부의 찬란한 치마폭도 있고,
무엇도 있고 무엇도 있고
바다에서처럼 어리벙벙하게
많이 있는 것은 없는가.

그러나 나는 한 가지
사람이 죽어
비록 형체는 없더라도 남기게 되는
반짝이는 것, 흔들리는 것은
꽃비늘로 환하게 둘러쓸 것을
마흔 한해 동안 고향 앞바다 보고
제일 많이 배운 바이니라.

What I Learned from the Sea

By the sea near my home,
the poplars rustle their leaves
whispering *Not a dream,*
and the brilliant, flowing folds
of the widow's skirt incite
delirium. There is all this
and all that, but nothing
of such bewildering abundance
as the sea.

But the one thing I have learned
most repeatedly from watching the sea
by my home for these forty-one years
is how to take the flower scales
and burnish bright the gleaming
or swaying that remains, the trace
when a person dies.

햇볕을 보며

지금 손사래로 막는
넘치는 햇빛이건만
돌아서면 뒷고개에도 와
부끄럽고 간지러워라.

그리고 내가 미처 모르는
아랍圈에도 赤道 근처에도
이글이글 타며 곤두박질치고 있고
눈 덮인 시베리아 벌판에도
오들오들 떨며 감싸고 있는

이 햇볕은 골고루 내려
바람의 伴奏로 한결
이 세상을 밝게 하네.

그러나 어제의 흘러간
또는 내일의 찬란한 햇볕은
하나도 존재하지 않고
오직 오늘의 햇볕만을 느끼는
위태롭고 막막한 이 한때!

Looking at the Sunlight

Though it is the very sunlight
that floods past my waving hands,
when I turn around, shyly
it tickles the back of my neck.

On places unknown to me—
Arab lands, the regions of the equator—
it tumbles headlong, blazing,
or on the vast, snow-covered
Siberian plain, trembling cold
it covers, protecting:

This sunlight descends
evenly with the wind,
bright on the world.

But of yesterday's fled
or tomorrow's brilliant
sun there is no trace;
only the sensation of today's
at this perilously empty moment.

아지랭이

스무살 무렵엔
웬 아지랭이가
그렇게 울었던지 몰라

고개 하나만 넘으면
바로 네 집이련만
벼락속까지 뚫고 갈
내 힘을 막으면서 죽이면서
머리를 풀고 울었던지 몰라.

아, 몰라야 몰라야,
그래놓고 나더니
오늘은 그 아지랭이가
어느새 마흔 살로 늙어
눈에는 눈꼽도 낀 채
나를 대신하여 다시 울고 있어라.

Shimmering

At twenty
I little knew
why the shimmering air cried so.

Your house was there
just over one more hill.
Holding back the strength of mine
that would pierce to the thunder's core,
I still did not know
why it loosed its hair and wept.

I've no idea, none,
why today the shimmering air
has suddenly become forty
and once again in place of me
cries with rheumy eyes.

小曲

노래밖에 모른다 해도
귀뚜라미가 옮기는 가녀린 발이
달빛 그늘을 짓밟고 깔아뭉개고
그렇게 한다고는 혹시 생각하지 않는가.

이 한밤
나혼자 쉬는 한숨이
사랑하는 잠든 사람의
어깨 위에 어느새
살이 아픈 뼈가 아픈
천 근의 무게되어 얹혀 있는데!

Small Song

We might agree the cricket knows
nothing but its singing,
but might it seem it will crush
the moonlit shadow where it sets
its frail feet and moves about?

The sigh I let
escape me this night
has settled on my love's shoulders,
a thousand-weight
pain of flesh, of bone.

별

차마 끊을 수 없어
반짝이는 인연인가,
손가락 사이 사이
빠져나간 별의 거리,
메울 수 없는 無力을
이미 울지 않는다.

오로지 감추기엔
불과 같은 죽음이여,
또한 드러내기엔
부끄러운 목숨이여,
그 거리 합쳐진 듯 갈라진 듯
銀河水는 흐른다.

가슴 울렁거려
내 자리잡지 못하고
하나 아닌 그리움
헤아리지 못하여
밤 人生...언덕에도 오르네,
시궁창에 빠지네.

Stars

It is a bond that gleams
because it cannot ever be broken?
The distance to the stars
that slip away between my fingers:
powerless to fill it,
I cannot lament.

Death too much like fire
only to be hidden,
life too shameful
to reveal,
and the Milky Way,
opening, closing the space between.

Heart skips,
cannot hold my position;
longing for not one,
beyond reckoning;
life at night . . . I climb
the hill, tumble into a cesspool.

산에서

그 곡절 많은 사랑은
기쁘던가 아프던가.

젊어 한창때
그냥 좋아서 어쩔 줄 모르던 기쁨이거든
여름날 헐떡이는 녹음에 묻혀들고
中年들어 肝臟이 저려오는 아픔이거든
가을날 울음빛 단풍에 젖어들거라.

진실로 산이 겪는 사철 속에
아른히 어린 우리 한평생

그가 다스리는 시냇물로
여름엔 시원하고
가을엔 시려오느니

사랑을 기쁘다고만 할 것이냐,
아니면 아프다고만 할 것이냐.

By the Mountain

That love with so many
turns to it; was it
happy, in the end, or sad?

It was nothing but joy,
no way to know the difference,
so glad for it in youthful prime.
Let that remain buried in the breathless leafy shade
of summer. In middle life,
let the piercing hurt of it
be drenched in the weeping colors
of autumn days.

Truly the four seasons
the mountain endures
inscribe our lifetimes.

The streams it watches over
run cool in summer,
turn cold in winter,

so shall we try to say that love
gladdens, or does it hurt?

사랑은

사랑은 개나리 환한
꽃가지 사이로 왔다가
이 겨울
허전한 팔가슴, 빈 가지 사이로
나를 달래는 빛깔인가, 희부옇게
눈이 내리면서,
그 뒷모습만 보이면서,
벌이 날개째로 우는 날은
다시 섭섭해 돌아올 것도 같은
그러한 표정으로
아, 결국은 사라지면서.

As for Love

Love appeared
between the blossoms
of forsythia
and then in winter's
empty embrace,
between the bare branches
while snow fell gentle,
a hazy white that might have calmed me,
it turned its back;
only in the end
when the bees began to buzz
and it seemed about to return
for pity of me, it vanished.

病後에

봄이 오는도다.
풀어버린 머리로다.
달래나물처럼 헹구어지는
쌍긋한 뒷맛
이제 피는 좀 식어
제자리 제대로 돌 것이로다.

눈여겨 볼 것이로다, 촉트는 풀잎,
가려운 흙살이 터지면서
약간은 아픈 氣도 있으면서
아, 그러면서 기쁘면서...
모든 살아 있는 것이
兄뻘로 보이는 넉넉함이로다.

땅에는 목숨뿌리를 박고
햇빛에 바람에
쉬다가 놀다가
하늘에는 솟으려는
가장 크면서 가장 작으면서
천지여!
어쩔 수 어쩔 수 없는
찬란한 몸짓이로다.

After an Illness

Spring is coming.
Like hair just untied.
Savor of garlic greens
that clean the palate.
The blood has cooled, now,
and will flow as it should.

Notice the buds, small steeples,
where the earth, sensitive as skin,
breaks just open
to a dull pain
mixed with delight.
Generous bounty makes all living things
seem like an elder brother.

Earth-rooted life,
sky-reaching to play or rest
with sunlight and wind,
great heaven and tiny earth, your
brilliant gesture that cannot be
stopped.

산에 가면

산에 가면
우거진 나무와 풀의
후텁지근한 냄새,

혼령도 눈도 코도 없는 것의
흙냄새까지 서린
아, 여기다, 하고 눕고 싶은
목숨의 골짜기 냄새,

한 동안을 거기서
내 몸을 쉬다가 오면
쉬던 그때는 없던 내 정신이
비로소 풀빛을 띠면서
나뭇잎 반짝거림을 띠면서
내 몸 전체에서
정신의 그릇을 넘는
후텁지근한 냄새를 내게 한다.

Going to the Mountain

When I go to the mountain
the scent is warm and moist
of trees and lush grasses;

a scent suffused with the smell of earth,
of something without soul or eyes or nose;
scent of the valley of my existence,
where I long to say Yes, here it is!
and lay myself down;

where if I rest
my body for a little while,
my spirit, absent
while I lay at rest, will take the color
of the grasses, bright glitter on leaves,
and from my body,
overflowing the vessel of my spirit,
let flow its scent, moist, and warm.

섬을 보는 자리

그의 형제와
그의 사촌들을 더불고 있듯이
바람받이 잘하고
햇살받이 잘하며
어린 섬들이 의좋게 논다.

어떤 때는
구슬을 줍듯이 머리를 수그리고
어떤 때는
고개 재껴 티없이 웃는다.

그중의 어떤 누이는
치맛살 펴 춤추기도 하고
그중의 어떤 동생은
뜀박질로 다가오기도 한다.

바라건대 하느님이여.
우리들의 나날은
늘 이와 같은
공일날로 있게 하소서.

Place Where I Look at Islands

As if with brothers and sisters,
as if with cousins too,
delighting in the wind,
joyous in the sun's light,
the young islands play quite happily.

At times they may seem to bow their heads
as if to pick up beads,
while at other times they toss their heads back
and laugh out innocently.

One sister in the bunch
spreads her skirt as if to dance,
while a younger one makes as if to run,
leaping forward as he comes.

O hear me, Heavenly Father.
Let our days too
be days of rest
always such as these.

追憶에서 16

우리 고향 八浦 앞바다에는
친이모도 빠져 죽고
먼 일가뻘 되는 숙모도 빠져 죽고
또 딴 사람들도 몇몇 귀한 목숨을 바쳤다.
그들은 왜 자살이라는 것을 택하여
삶의 마감을 닫은 것일까.
거기에 아슬한 꿈의 파편이 묻어
살맛나게 하는 引力이 있지 않았을까.
아마도 죽을 그 임시에는
바다가 꽃밭으로 보일 것에
틀림없으리라고 짚어보았다.
그래서 한결같이 고무신을
곱게 벗어 두고 들어갔던가.
아, 서러운 이유는 다
어디론가 어느샌가 속속들이 잊고
크낙한 아름다움에
푹신 취해서 젖어들고 있었다고 풀이해 보았다.
그 아름다운 바다가
그러나 내 나이 쉰이 넘은 눈에는
시들하고 멋대가리 없는 것으로
어느새 둔갑하고 있었다.

Recollection 16

In the sea near P'alp'o my home,
one aunt drowned herself.
A distant aunt had drowned herself too,
and others; their precious lives they gave away.
Suicide: why choose *that*?
What shattered dream fragment
made them long so to end their lives?
Did the sea resemble a flower garden?
Was that the reason they all removed their shoes
before they leaped?
I tried to imagine
they had forgotten the faraway,
already distant causes of their own sorrows,
drenched, intoxicated as they were by that greater beauty.
But to my eyes now I have passed fifty, the sea
has become a dull thing, and plain.

이 가을 들면서

올 여름은
삼베 홑이불로 살더위를 가렸더니
이 가을 들면서
千里 끝 햇빛도 서늘하게 몸에 닿고

올 여름은
마늘酒로 입 天障 가셨더니
이 가을 들면서
머리위 바람도 맑게 흐르네.

Autumn Coming

This summer
I shielded myself from the heat
with a thin hempen weave,
and now as autumn at last draws near
sunlight a thousand *li* away
touches my body just gently;

and having rinsed my mouth
this summer
with garlic wine,
as autumn draws near
the winds above my head flow clear.

잠이 먼 밤에

새도 바람소리도
잠결 언저리로 몰려간 뒤
山이 하는 기척은
이제는 뼈골에 사무치는
물소리 하나다.

짐승보다도 더러운 핏줄
내 高血壓도 맑혀주었으면……
그런 건 모르겠다, 그런 건 모르겠다,
山 공부나 다시 하거라,
그렇게 밖에는 들리지 않는
섭섭한 섭섭한 물소리.

나만 빼돌려 놓고
아내의 숨소리도 아이들의 그것도
함께 휘말아 가누나.
……참말로 그러긴가.

A Night When Sleep Is Far

After the sounds of wind and birds
have crowded away to the edge of sleep,
still in my memories of the mountain
there lingers the sound of water,
piercing to my bones.

Veins revolting as some disgusting beast;
if it might cleanse my fragile vessels . . .
but the only thing the dispiriting sound
of the water tells me, Back to your study
of mountains. I don't know about that other;
I don't know.

Holding me aside,
meddling with the sound of my wife
and my children breathing . . .
How could you?

Translators' Epilogue

I first met Pak Chaesam in 1973, when my translation of his poem "Untitled" received the Commendation Award in the annual contest sponsored by the *Korea Times*. He attended the award ceremony, expressed cordial thanks for my interest in his work, and invited me to go out for a drink sometime.

We did eventually have our evening together, some months later, but for a long interval afterward, we lost touch. I kept reading his poems, though, drawn by qualities that I still find it difficult to describe directly. Emily Dickinson's work and life, her role as something of an inside-outsider to the life of the town of Amherst and New England literary culture, has seemed the closest analogue.

During one of my trips to Seoul in 1996, I heard that Pak Chaesam's health had taken an ominous turn. I called him and we talked for a while, but he told me he did not feel quite up to a meeting then. "Next time you are in Seoul," he suggested. But only a few months later, he was gone.   —DRM

Unlike my cotranslator David McCann, I never met Pak Chaesam during his lifetime. In fact, it probably would not have occurred to me to read his poems had it not been for those few lines in his poem "Untitled" about the train reaching the height of its fever by the orchards near Taegu. My very first obsession with poetry had been with a verse about a train, though not a provincial passenger coach as in that poem, but the Parisian Metro that spews out an apparition of faces, "petals on a wet black bough," in Ezra Pound. Where Pound himself stressed the imagistic instant, of a thing outward "darting into" a thing inward, I used to relish, instead, the sense of utter anonymity of an urbanite, which I had considered myself living in metropolitan Seoul in the 1970s and 1980s, when the extensive subway lines were first laid throughout the city. I had little in me to relate to the world of shimmering waves and seaweed breezes in a seaside town. The quiet chamber of Pak's lyricism, the stillness, for instance, of a courtyard through which the first raindrop on a plantain leaf resonates, was just as foreign to me as the "unfolding of the sea in the other shores of the Pacific" was to Pak Chaesam. But had I not ventured into the foreignness of a fishing village boy's melancholy, I probably would never have learned what makes a boy a lyric poet. In the case of Pak Chaesam, it was neither the rolling bellows, nor the marine spirit hanging fearlessly at the tip of a mast, but the fluttering of the widow's skirt at the edge of a cliff as she threw herself into the depths of the sea that nurtured the yearning of a poet in a boy. As I read and translated his poems, I saw, emerging from the place quite different from the Parisian Metro, an apparition of faces—faces of women buried in the flowing folds of the skirt.

In looking back, this project has been for me a learning process, not only in translating poetry, but also in reading poetry. For translation is about difference, and much of my work here has involved negotiating differences—between the clamor in what I knew of late twentieth-century Korean poetry and the tranquility in Pak Chaesam's world and between David's splendid reading and my stubborn insistence on rereading. I thank my friend and my teacher David McCann for having given me the chance to see what I would never have otherwise seen, and for having allowed me to learn from differences.   —JS

George Seferis: Collected Poems (1924–1995), translated, edited, and introduced by Edmund Keeley and Philip Sherrard

Collected Poems of Lucio Piccolo, translated and edited by Brian Swann and Ruth Feldman

C. P. Cavafy: Selected Poems, translated by Edmund Keeley and Philip Sherrard and edited by George Savidis

Benny Andersen: Collected Poems, translated by Alexander Taylor

Selected Poetry of Andrea Zanzotto, edited and translated by Ruth Feldman and Brian Swann

Poems of René Char, translated and annotated by Mary Ann Caws and Jonathan Griffin

Selected Poems of Tudor Arghezi, translated by Michael Impey and Brian Swann

"The Survivor" and Other Poems by Tadeusz Rózewicz, translated and introduced by Magnus J. Krynski and Robert A. Maguire

"Harsh World" and Other Poems by Angel González, translated by Donald D. Walsh

Ritsos in Parentheses, translations and introduction by Edmund Keeley

Salamander: Selected Poems of Robert Marteau, translated by Anne Winters

Angelos Sikelianos: Selected Poems, translated and introduced by Edmund Keeley and Philip Sherrard

Dante's "Rime," translated by Patrick S. Diehl

Selected Later Poems of Marie Luise Kaschnitz, translated by Lisel Mueller

Osip Mandelstam's "Stone," translated and introduced by Robert Tracy

The Dawn Is Always New: Selected Poetry of Rocco Scotellaro, translated by Ruth Feldman and Brian Swann

Sounds, Feelings, Thoughts: Seventy Poems by Wisława Szymborska, translated and introduced by Magnus J. Krynski and Robert A. Maguire

The Man I Pretend to Be: "The Colloquies" and Selected Poems of Guido Gozzano, translated and edited by Michael Palma, with an introductory essay by Eugenio Montale

D'Après Tout: Poems by Jean Follain, translated by Heather McHugh

Songs of Something Else: Selected Poems of Gunnar Ekelöf, translated by Leonard Nathan and James Larson

The Little Treasury of One Hundred People, One Poem Each, compiled by Fujiwara No Sadaie and translated by Tom Galt

The Ellipse: Selected Poems of Leonardo Sinisgalli, translated by W. S. Di Piero

The Difficult Days by Roberto Sosa, translated by Jim Lindsey

Hymns and Fragments by Friedrich Hölderlin, translated and introduced by Richard Sieburth

The Silence Afterwards: Selected Poems of Rolf Jacobsen, translated and edited by Roger Greenwald

Rilke: Between Roots, selected poems rendered from the German by Rika Lesser

In the Storm of Roses: Selected Poems by Ingeborg Bachmann, translated, edited, and introduced by Mark Anderson

Birds and Other Relations: Selected Poetry of Dezső Tandori, translated by Bruce Berlind

Brocade River Poems: Selected Works of the Tang Dynasty Courtesan Xue Tao, translated and introduced by Jeanne Larsen

The True Subject: Selected Poems of Faiz Ahmed Faiz, translated by Naomi Lazard

My Name on the Wind: Selected Poems of Diego Valeri, translated by Michael Palma

Aeschylus: The Suppliants, translated by Peter Burian

Foamy Sky: The Major Poems of Miklós Radnóti, selected and translated by Zsuzanna Ozváth and Fredrick Turner

La Fontaine's Bawdy: Of Libertines, Louts, and Lechers, translated by Norman R. Shapiro

A Child Is Not a Knife: Selected Poems of Göran Sonnevi, translated and edited by Rika Lesser

George Seferis: Collected Poems, Revised Edition, translated, edited, and introduced by Edmund Keeley and Philip Sherrard

C. P. Cavafy: Collected Poems, Revised Edition, translated and introduced by Edmund Keeley and Philip Sherrard, and edited by George Savidis

Selected Poems of Shmuel HaNagid, translated from the Hebrew by Peter Cole

The Late Poems of Meng Chiao, translated and introduced by David Hinton

Leopardi: Selected Poems, translated and introduced by Eamon Gennan

Through Naked Branches: Selected Poems of Tarjei Vesaas, translated and edited by Roger Greenwald

The Complete Odes and Satires of Horace, translated with introduction and notes by Sidney Alexander

Selected Poems of Solomon Ibn Gabirol, translated by Peter Cole

Puerilities: Erotic Epigrams of The Greek Anthology, translated by Daryl Hine

Night Journey by María Negroni, translated and introduced by Anne Twitty

Nothing Is Lost: Selected Poems by Edvard Kocbek, translated by Michael Scammell and Veno Taufer, and introduced by Michael Scammell

The Complete Elegies of Sextus Propertius, translated with introduction and notes by Vincent Katz

Knowing the East, by Paul Claudel, translated with introduction and notes by James Lawler

Enough to Say It's Far: Selected Poems of Pak Chaesam, translated by David R. McCann and Jiwon Shin